Garden Chrysanthemums and First Mountain Snow
Zen Questions and Answers from Korea

GARDEN CHRYSANTHEMUMS
AND
FIRST MOUNTAIN SNOW

Zen Questions and Answers from Korea

Edited by
Ian Haight

Translated by
Hongjin Park and Eryn Reager

WHITE PINE PRESS / BUFFALO, NEW YORK

Published by
White Pine Press
P.O. Box 236, Buffalo, New York 14201
www.whitepine.org

Publication of this book was made possible by The Baroboin
Buddhist Foundation.

First Edition

Cover image: "Untitled," by Hyeon Jeong, 1992.

Printed and bound in the United States of America

ISBN 978-1-935210-19-1

Library of Congress Control Number: 2010925981

GARDEN CHRYSANTHEMUMS AND FIRST MOUNTAIN SNOW
Zen Questions and Answers from Korea

Table of Contents

Introduction / 9

Editor's Note / 13

Part I

Questions and Answers with Zen Master Taewŏn / 17

Part II

Selected Conversations Between Master Taewŏn
and Other Korean Zen Masters / 49

Part III

Questions and Answers with Ten Zen Masters of Korea / 63

Important Figures in Korean Zen / 97

Dictionary of Terms / 107

INTRODUCTION

Ian Haight

Korea is one of the few countries in the world where Living Zen Buddhism is practiced. Living Zen is a Zen tradition of directly enlightening practitioners to their original nature. It is different from Literal Zen, which is based on book learning. In Literal Zen, Masters and practitioners teach and learn enlightenment by a literal description of it found in sutras or ancient manuscripts. By contrast, Living Zen Masters lead practitioners closer to their original nature.

A true adherence to Living Zen does not stop there. One must make his or her daily life the embodiment of enlightenment to be truly called a practice of Living Zen. Even after an experience of enlightenment, if one's daily life does not reflect the wisdom of enlightenment, the life is not a Living Zen practice.

This book is a collection of questions posed to Korea's elder Living Zen Masters, and their answers. Funny, irreverent, serious, humble, wise, compassionate, poetic, and centered—these are terms that describe only partially the Zen Masters' answers in this book. Part I contains questions posed to Zen Master Taewŏn, and his answers. Part II contains excerpts of conversations between Zen Master Taewŏn and other Korean Zen Masters. Several of these conversations were used as tests to determine Zen Master Taewon's enlightenment; his responses led to dharma transmission from Zen Master Chŏn'gang. Part III of this text contains selections of questions and answers posed to ten of Korea's Living Zen Masters. The difference in tone among these Zen Masters' answers—deserving of contemplation, deceptively simple— paints a portrait of personality among these Zen Masters, and how they live and teach enlightenment.

Comparatively few texts on Korean Buddhism exist in

English translation. It is hoped this book will give a lively introductory voice to the spirit of Korea's Living Zen tradition.

Editor's Note

I have been asked by Master Taewŏn's fellow disciples to explain why I agreed to edit this manuscript. I skimmed through the manuscript upon it being handed to me, and I was struck by what I believe readers will be most attracted to in this book: the idea that Zen permeates life. We find in this book dynamic expressions that touch both neophytes, and those who are long-time acquaintances with Zen. Zen is more than an esoteric religion of Asia, perhaps made into a culture fetish by westerners; Zen is something that helps define our families—how we see one another as human beings not only in our respective communities, but across the globe. We find guidance in how to observe ourselves, how to think with ease, and depth. We find that a mind centered in an immediate present has no location, but scintillates through reality. This manuscript surprised me, reminded me of wisdom I already knew in a welcoming manner, as well as introduced me to unfamiliar perspectives. I believe this book will move others in the same way it has moved me.

Readers of this collection will notice that questions directed to Master Taewŏn, his answers, and his conversations with other Zen Masters occupy a significant portion of the text. His Zen centers have fostered the creation of this book, and within Korea, the numbers of those who practice his form of Living Zen continue to grow. This book can be taken as a cross-section of conversations with Korea's elder Living Zen Masters, with special emphasis on the words of Zen Master Taewŏn.

Finally, many hands have participated in the creation of

the manuscript, through to its final draft. I would like to especially thank Chinsŏng Chuyŏng Yun, without whose help this book could not have been completed.

—Ian Haight, Editor

White clouds drift over Mt. Mudung,
the reservoir water overflows.

Chinčh'ol! Bring tea!
Shall we enjoy this moment,
facing one another, while sipping warm tea?

—Offering incense to the Buddha,
Zen Master Taewŏn

DE 4334
BE 3028
AD Nov. 20th, 2001

Part I

Questions and Answers with Zen Master Taewŏn

How should I follow a rugged road?

Go straight.

❋

What is a practitioner supposed to do?

Whatever you do, never leave the royal throne.

❋

What is the truth? And what is that which is without even a trace of truth?

Seven times seven is forty-nine.

What is the distance between father and son?

It is the distance between the sea and its salty taste.

✸

Who is the one that knows neither good nor evil?

One who does not ask that kind of question.

Can this person know there is no such thing as transcendence?

(The master shows the answer with silence.)

Are you showing the answer to me now?

Have some tea.

Who is the one that has transcended the Buddha?

It is always evident.
So, one who asks cannot perceive it.

⁂

How do enlightened people transcend their bodies?

When a sheriff passes through, his horse passes also.

⁂

Why can't a person catch a fish even after spending
an entire day at the lake?

If there is anyone who caught a fish,
tell me his name.

How can I attain true dharma?

If it is attained, it can't be true dharma.

❋

All other Zen centers are prosperous with hundreds of disciples. Why aren't there many practitioners in your center, which you say succeeds to the authoritative lineage of the Buddha?

A mountain that has four seasons is good for all the animals to live on because there are many trees and flowers. But at the peaks of the Himalayas, even birds rarely approach.

Where is the Zen Master when he is in deep sleep
without dreams?

As the wind dies down in the universe,
what a clear divulgence there is!

❀

What is the original purpose of Buddhist dharma?

As the sun and moon explode, the sea brightens.

❀

Your Buddhist name is Taewŏn.
What does "Tae" mean?

It means enlightenment without inside or outside.

Then, what about "Wŏn"?

It means that original natures are boundless
and never interfere with one another.

What are the traditions of your sect?

Today, after having breakfast, I came to the Zen
center. I met people and talked with them.

How is it before one thought arises?

Two thoughts.

What is your most profound place, Master?

The body is not in any way covered,
but not one in millions can see it.

Why isn't there a shadow
when two mirrors face each other?

Clouds float and water runs.

How is it when the mirrors
are pulverized into nothing?

Mt. Mudŭng is red in the fall and white in winter.

Who are you closer to,
the Buddha or the Patriarchs?

Even those names sound like enemies.

●

Who is the person that feels no envy?

Turning each page brings one to the end of a book.

●

Can a book impart the salient features of a sect?

In midsummer,
people open doors and hang bamboo blinds.

Whose song do you sing
and whose dharma do you succeed?

The round moon over the southern sea
is the full moon over Yudal Mountain in Mokp'o.

　

When one gets enlightenment and the mind
becomes stable, to whom is the virtue attributed?

Can it truly be a virtue
if it is attributed to someone?

What about when there isn't even
a thought of virtue?

This kind of person wouldn't ask
with your beggar's voice.

Since the Buddha, how have Zen Masters asked
and answered questions about Zen?

Paektu Mountain in the north is covered with snow,
royal azalea blossoms are in full bloom
on Mt. Halla in the south

What do you do when the only way is too long?

If it is too long, how can it be the only way?

What is the only way?

A woman dances at the crossroads.

Before the mind moves, where is the dharma?

It's like wind in the sky before it blows.

✳

What were you before you received a human body?

Well, I was looking for a 170 million-year-old egg,
but there's still no way to find it.

On his way to visit the enlightened layman, Pang-gŏsa, Master Tan-ha, came across Pang-gŏsa's daughter and asked, "Is your father home?" She put her herb basket on the ground and stood still. What did it mean when she put her basket down and stood still?

She was clear with everything.

When Master Tan-ha asked her again, she picked up the basket and went away. How was it then?

She was clear with everything.

If the smallest tip of a hair is only dust,
how is it when there is not even a hair?

Right now, is there nothing, or is there something?

❀

All beings have lost their original nature and so are subject to samsara. How can they recover their original nature?

Bring me an icicle hanging on the eaves
in midsummer.

It is said that the use of the mind belongs to the present. Then what about when the mind is not used at all?

Even all the Buddhas
of the three periods cannot see it.

❀

What are the fundamentals of Zen?

Cows eat grass.

❀

What was the message
when Buddha held up a flower?

The sound of chimes.

What is the supreme truth?

The incense smoke between
candles looks like thread.

⚜

Here, if you say you entered, I'll hit you. If you say
you didn't, I'll hit you too. Tell me right now.

(shouts) Huh!

I can't find a teacher anywhere in the world.
Who is the master of heaven and earth?

Can there be a servant without a Master?

What shall I do?

Counterbalancing is done only on a scale.

I'll accept what you say.

Even if you speak the dharma which transcends
Sŏkkamoni Buddha, you still cannot avoid Taewŏn's
cudgel. How will you avoid it?

What would you do if you met a great general?

That would be the most comfortable situation.

How is it when a wagon stops
but the cow that pulls it doesn't?

Forget about whether the wagon stops or not.
In which direction did you say the cow moved?

(There was no answer,
so the Master hit the student.)

❀

When the oars stop and the wind calms,
how can I get to the hill?

Forget about getting to the hill.
Show me where I can take a step.

(A visitor bowed to Master Taewŏn and took a seat.)

A truly dexterous person
doesn't do that kind of thing.

What are the traditions of your sect, Master?

There is no outside though I use the mind,
and no inside though I do not use it.

Who is the guest in the Master?

The beggar who asks.

Who is the Master in the guest?

From where are you asking?

Who is the host within the host?

Is it possible not to see?

Who is the guest inside the guest?

Someone like you who, asking,
wanders here and there.

Is the rock on the mountain inside your mind
or outside your mind?

(shouts) Huh!
Don't discriminate between inside and outside.
When responding naturally in the present, without
limits, everything is appropriate. This is enjoyment
where there's no enjoyment.

❁

Would you show me your greatest compassion?

It's just been shown.

Tell me every koan in one word.

Mountains are high.

꽃

How can people become Buddha,
freed from ignorance and delusion?

It is revealed clearly, so there is nothing to say. But
for your sake I will tell you: A fish jumps out of water
and disappears into it; a bolt of lightning flashes in
the empty sky and disappears into it. Where do your
good or evil thoughts appear and disappear? (The
Master shows the answer with silence.) In fact, com-
pared to this, seeing something in front of your eyes
is more difficult. Have you perceived it?

(The questioner says nothing.)

Even your green leggings are telling you.
My compassion and ability are revealed.

If I killed a thief, I would be breaking Buddha's precepts; but if I didn't, I would be disobeying the order
of the king. What would you do, Master?

Forget about all that
and show me what you have that can be stolen.

How can I teach people not to be attached
to the Buddha's teaching that "mind is Buddha?"

How are you speaking now?

What is true dharma?

I don't know anything called "true dharma."

What is "not knowing anything called true dharma?"

I don't know that, either.

What is "I don't know that, either?"

True dharma.

What is the stage without a fault?

If you say "stage," there must be a fault.

(After the student looked at a picture
of Mt. Paektu on the wall)
How did this huge mountain get inside the room?

Where is outside?

How will it be when the Maitreya comes?

Truly, it will be just like this.

What is "mysterious existence of true emptiness"?

What is it like now?

How far is it between mysterious existence
and true emptiness?

(Master Taewŏn scratches his head.)

❀

What is the only way of the Ancient Buddha?

Show me something that is not the only way.

What is the Buddha nature?

Your mother.

✻

What is the eternal stream of life and death?

What is the eternal stream of life and death?

What does it mean to be free from the eternal stream of life and death, to enjoy one's original nature?

What does it mean to be free from the eternal stream of life and death, to enjoy one's original nature?

Tell me words which do not exist.

Only one who listens without listening can hear.

❁

Before Master Pŏmnyung met the 4th Patriarch Tosin, Pŏmnyung received offerings from devas, birds, and other animals. Why was this?

It was a time of extreme devotion.

After Master Pŏmnyung met the 4th Patriarch Tosin, the offerings from animals and devas stopped. Why was this?

At last, for him,
there were not even the words, "Buddhist dharma."

What is your one-pointed teaching of enlightenment?

Haven't you heard it?

How is it when there isn't even
the necessity to return to original nature?

How is it?

Where is Bodhi situated?

From where are you asking?

How can wandering people
return to their original home?

What is asking right now?

❀

Do you sleep?

Yes, I do.

Do you have dreams?

What is a dream?

The saying "mind is Buddha" deceives people. But how do you instruct those who don't follow the paths of the Buddha or patriarchs?

Where and how did that saying originate?

How can people transcend the Buddha
and the idea that they have transcended?

A sparrow plays at the end of eaves and a cat plays in the garden. Is this transcendence or non-transcendence?

(The questioner remains silent)

Come, have some tea.

Part II

Conversations Between Zen Master Taewŏn and Other Korean Zen Masters

Dialogue with Zen Master Kyŏngbong

In 1956, Master Taewŏn heard that Master Kyŏngbong was staying at Kŭngnakam Hermitage of T'ongdo Temple in Yangsan, and so went there to pay him a visit. It was late fall and Master Kyŏngbong was picking persimmons in the garden with his stick. Master Taewŏn bowed to Master Kyŏngbong and stood in front of him:

Kyŏngbong: Where are you from?

Taewŏn: I am from Honam.

Kyongbŏng: What have you studied?

Taewŏn: I have studied Zen.

Kyŏngbong: What is Zen?

Taewŏn: (At this very moment Kyongbŏng was

pulling a persimmon from his stick) The persimmon
is red.

Kyŏngbong: Then do you know the dharma?

Taewŏn: If it can be known, it is not the dharma.

Dialogue with Master Chŏn'gang 1

Tonggwang Temple, a large temple in Kwangju City, was once used as an administrative office of the Chogye Order of Korean Buddhism. After his dharma talk during the summer of 1957, Master Chŏn'gang was resting there in the dharma hall. When Master Taewŏn was passing by, Master Chŏn'gang called him in:

Chŏn'gang: Today, I gave a dharma talk on Bodhidharma's "I don't know" koan, but nobody answered. How would you answer?

Taewŏn: (He approached Master Chŏn'gang without a word, pulled out a long hair from a mole on the master's neck, and walked away).

Chŏn'gang: There's a murderer here! (He followed after Master Taewŏn yelling loudly.)

Dialogue with Zen Master Chŏn'gang 2

In the harvest season of 1959, Master Taewŏn was acting as a servant for Master Chŏn'gang at Ŭnjŏk Temple in Kunsan. One day, while resting after lunch, he came across Master Chŏn'gang in the dharma hall's garden:

Chŏn'gang: Tell me the mysterious wisdom of the empty and serene original nature.

Taewŏn: "Just like this," I talk with you.

Chŏn'gang: Tell me the empty and serene state of the mysterious wisdom.

Taewŏn: While talking with you, I am "just like this."

Chŏn'gang: What is the stage of talking "just like this?"

Taewŏn: A wise king knows and responds to everything without leaving his royal seat.

Dialogue with Zen Master Chŏn'gang 3

A few days later Master Chŏn'gang and Master Taewŏn spoke again:

Chŏn'gang: Tell me the stage of great equality, of mysterious wisdom, and the "empty and serene" state.

Taewŏn: The sun in the sky is white and the autumn water is clean. It would be a demon's discourse to say the Buddha is superior to all beings, or all beings are inferior to the Buddha.

Dialogue with Zen Master Muksan

Master Taewŏn once visited Master Muksan in Seoul during the summer of 1963. Master Muksan asked Master Taewŏn about this poem by Pang-gŏsa:

North, south, east, west, up, and down gathered together
and learned "not-doing" in every behavior.
This is the test that distinguishes the Buddha;
everything returns home after enlightenment.

Muksan: What is the gathering of the ten directions?

Taewŏn: You cannot stick even a tiny needle into it.

Muksan: What is learning "not-doing" in everything?

Taewŏn: Responding without inside or outside.

Muksan: What is the test that distinguishes the Buddha?

Taewŏn: The chrysanthemums in the front garden are beautiful and the first mountain snow is white.

Muksan: What is returning to the empty mind after enlightenment?

Taewŏn: How can this stage be clear when only listening to dogs and cats?

Dialogue with Master Sungsan I

Master Taewŏn met Master Sungsan at the ceremony to celebrate the completion of Kuryong Temple in the summer of 1989. The excerpts below are taken from a long conversation they shared. Outside their room, shouting, slapping, the thudding of thrown objects, and finally loud laughter could be heard. Others who were waiting to see Master Sungsan wondered what was going on inside. When the door opened, Master Sungsan called in those who accompanied Master Taewŏn and told them they were blessed to have Master Taewŏn as their teacher.

Sungsan: Tell me the answer to the koan, "Three pounds of hemp."

Taewŏn: (He slaps Master Sungsan on the cheek.)

Sungsan: You ask me.

Taewŏn: Tell me the answer to the koan, "Three

pounds of hemp."

Sungsan: (He slaps Master Taewŏn on the cheek.)

⬤

Taewŏn: You once wrote me, "Upon a white stone within a green mountain, true face is completely revealed." What is your true face?

Sungsan: (Pointing to a chair) A chair. What is true face?

Taewŏn: The nose on your face is a little high, and the wall stands upright behind your back.

Taewŏn: Don't speak, don't stay silent, don't move or be still, but answer!

Sungsan: (shouts loudly) Huh! If I asked you to answer without speaking, staying silent, moving, or being still, what would you do?

Taewŏn: What answer do you ask me to make without speaking, staying silent, moving, or being still?

Sungsan: No. Tell me again.

Taewŏn: Speaking! Silence! Moving! Stillness!

✳

Sungsan: (Pointing at a peeled persimmon on a small tea table) If you say this is a persimmon, you are wrong, but if you say it is not, you are also wrong.

Answer me!

Taewŏn: (He immediately flipped the table upside down.)

❀

Sungsan: (When discussing the koan "Namjon kills a cat") If you had been there, how would you have saved the cat?

Taewŏn: I would have hugged a pillar.

Sungsan: You're wrong. You don't know anything.

Taewŏn: Master, why are you so angry? Ask me once more.

Sungsan: If you had been there, how would you have

saved the cat?

Taewŏn: I'd have stuck my neck out in front of Master Namjŏn.

Sungsan: That's it. Why didn't you say that before?

(Later Master Taewŏn said to himself, "But there's no difference between hugging a pillar and sticking out one's neck....")

Part III

Questions and Answers
with Ten Zen Masters of Korea

These conversations took place with lay people
who came to visit the respective Masters.
The conversations took place from
October 1998 to February 1999.

Dialogue with Zen Master Hyeam

I came here empty-handed.

Put it down.

I have nothing. What do I have to put down?

Then, take it with you.

Who is the person whose stage transcends the Buddha?

A farmer plowing a field in the village.

Because of Korea's financial crisis, people's lives have become more difficult. Burglary and theft are rapidly increasing. It has been said that if one kills a criminal, that person goes against the precepts, but if he doesn't, he would be breaking the law of the king. What do you think of this?

With respect to dharma, even a pin-hole leak is unacceptable, but outside the dharma, a horse and carriage can go anywhere.

❀

Eminent teachers of the past constantly emphasized, "If you meet the Buddha, kill him. If you meet a patriarch, kill him too." If you kill your parents, you can repent to the the Buddha, but if you kill the Buddha, to whom do you repent?

The answer is laid bare.

After you die, if someone asks, "What was Hyeam's dharma?" how should we answer?

I had a meal and slept.

Dialogue with Zen Master Posŏng

Has every monk of this temple drunk "a drop of the Chogye stream" in front of Song-gwang Temple?

I knew you from the moment you entered.

Did you attain the dharma of Chogye?

I don't know dharma.

Master, what truth did you see that leads to such a peaceful life on Mt. Chogye, with its fresh air and beautiful scenery?

I have fallen into a hole of shit.

In the secular world, sexual morality is a serious problem. They say that half of the teenage prosti- tutes are middle school students. How would you enlighten them?

All of us are living too far from our homes.

There is an old woman who always worries. When it rains, she worries about her daughter who sells straw shoes. When it's sunny, she worries about her other daughter who sells umbrellas. How would you relieve her from anxiety?

Think of only the daughter who sells umbrellas on rainy days, and the daughter who sells straw shoes on sunny days.

Dialogue with Zen Master Wŏndam

Master, you are so handsome. Why didn't you become a politician or public official?

What's better than being a monk? You have to research hard and write articles to earn your living, but we only have to beat the mokt'ak well.

How many beings have you saved so far?

Not a one. I couldn't save myself, either.

What kind of dharma have you taught?

I've done nothing but curse.

What kind of cursing?

Hey! Son of a bitch!

⁕

What kinds of people were Sŏkkamoni Buddha and
Bodhidharma?

Sŏkkamoni Buddha was a robber in India and
Bodhidharma was a swindler in China.

How about you, Master?

I am the same.

✻

I smoke a lot. But at fancy restaurants or country clubs, smoking areas are limited to small corners that have a "Smoking Area" sign. Sometimes I want to smoke while having a meal in a non-smoking area that has a fine view. What should I do?

Move.

✻

Many people have become poor due to the country's financial crisis. What alms should I give them?

A beggar lacks nothing.

○

I bought a cake for you, but on the way here, I saw a starving dog lying on the street and gave the cake to him instead.

You gave alms to the Buddha.

Dialogue with Zen Master Sŏong

If you came across a drunken man, how would you enlighten him?

Even a flashing blade against my neck is just the autumn wind.

What is the "everyday mind" that becomes one with the Tao?

While I drink tea and eat rice, time passes. When I see the mountains and the water, my mind is refreshed.

Last night, I had a fight with my wife. How should I behave myself this evening?

Knock first.

❄

I came here because this is the Ancient Buddha Monastic Training Center. But I can see only a gold Buddha statue, not the Ancient Buddha. Where is the Ancient Buddha?

Omi tea tastes good in summer. Drink a glass of omi tea.

(After drinking tea) I still can't see the Ancient Buddha.

It passed in front of you long ago.

·❀·

If an earthworm is cut in two, both of the pieces wriggle. In which piece does the Buddha nature exist?

That kind of question deserves 30 whacks from my stick.

But if an earthworm is cut in two, the pieces still wriggle. Why?

The four elements have not yet scattered.

If a snake is about to swallow a frog, should I save it or leave it alone?

If you save the frog, you will become blind. If you leave it alone, you won't be able to see either it or its shadow.

❀

Who is a true person?

One who doesn't tell a lie. If a person is honest his conscience is clean. And if his conscience is clean, he can be absolutely free. But politicians, businessmen, and government officials tell too many lies. Even priests tell lies.

The weather is sizzling hot these days. Please tell me the stage after nirvana.

I pull up my trousers and forget about the hot weather.

●

While coming here, I saw vines of arrowroot winding up a pine tree. What will happen to the vines if the tree falls down?

Huh, huh. In full daylight, you talk in your sleep.

●

I came from Seoul by train to learn about existence

and non-existence. It cost fifteen thousand won.

(To his attendant) Give this man some money to go back to Seoul.

❀

If a blind, deaf, and mute person came to you and begged for teaching, how would you enlighten him?

I would dance with him hand in hand.

There is a statute of the Buddha in a temporary building. What kind of miraculous power does that statute have?

You've already seen the power.

Dialogue with Zen Master Sŏngsu

Have the spiritual fruits ripened in Hwangdae Village?

Lay women offered too much money to the monks. Now they have all been corrupted.

When coming here, I saw birds singing in the old trees. They asked, "What will you do after you enter the forest?"

Funny. I enter a weed heap and you enter a forest.

Who is the person who leisurely enjoys everyday life after being enlightened to true nature?

A fan in the middle of winter.

Have you attained enlightenment?

Yesterday and today.

It is said that the Buddha is originally inside of us. Why then do you practice so hard and worship the Buddha so sincerely every day?

I was totally deceived by the Buddha.

Dialogue with Zen Master Chinje

Your face is not worthy of your fame.

Give me some pocket money.

What is your last name?

Right now.

What is the most precious and joyful thing?

The street sweepers of Pusan and the farmers of Kimhae.

84

There is a caldron in a very rich household. The rice in the caldron is not enough for three men, but far more than enough for a thousand. How is this possible?

If people fight it will not be enough, but if they share with one another it will be more than enough.

It is said that all the sounds in the world are the Buddha's sermons. Then, is the sound of defecating or urinating also the Buddha's sermons?

Yes.

What are the most indispensable accompaniments to meals at your Zen center?

Shouting and hitting.

Dialogue with Zen Master Sokchu

Where do all the Buddhas of past, present, and future exist?

On the back of a mother pig.

How is a mirror after it reflects light?

Dark.

Buddhist dharma is extremely profound. How should I practice and use my mind in everyday life?

They are not two.

※

What would you do if you came across an enlightened person?

I'd achieve supreme dharma.

※

When will the world obtain peace?

I'm just waiting for your mind to find contentment.

Who is the master in time before the universe was created?

I am here.

♦

After you enter nirvana, if someone asks what the essence of your enlightenment was, how should I answer?

When the vegetables withered during a drought, I watered the garden.

Dialogue with Zen Master Kosong

Where were you before you were conceived?

Sir, where are you now?

I don't understand. Please explain it to me again.

I don't know any more than you.

What is the Tao?

The mountains in front of you are showing them-selves just as they are. The clouds are in the sky, and water is in the bottle.

Does heaven or hell exist?

Yes.

Does the mind or the Buddha also exist?

Yes, they do.

But other Zen Masters have said consistently that all is nothingness and emptiness.

You have a wife, so you are "being," but monks don't, so they are "not being."

What are your special powers and how do you use them?

I get water to drink and prepare firewood.

Dialogue with Zen Master Sŏam

What is the majestic feature of T'aebaek Mountain?

Wind brings water sounds to the pillow, moonlight
moves a mountain's shadow to the bed.

What are precepts, meditation, and wisdom?

Here, there is no such useless furniture.

What do you teach to visitors?

I plow the field in the morning and rake in the evening.

While I was crossing the river this morning, I was confused about whether the bridge or the water was flowing. Which is correct?

The bridge runs, not the water.

Dialogue with Zen Master Sungsan

A man raised a baby goose in a bottle. It grew until it was too big for the bottle. Is there any way to get it out without breaking the bottle or injuring the bird?

(Suddenly in a loud voice) Mr. Lee!

Yes?

Come out.

What is the Buddha?

Kimch'i.

What is "the sword in a dream?"

A skeleton.

※

(It was about noon when the conversation finished. Master Sungsan ordered his attendant to prepare lunch.) It is said that the mind of three periods cannot be attained. Then, in which mind will you have your lunch?

I am just hungry.

Important Figures in Korean Zen

Zen Master Chŏn'gang

Master Chŏn'gang was born in Koksong, Chŏnnam Province, in 1898. Ordained at the age of sixteen in 1914, Master Chŏn'gang was well known for his strength of austere practice, and received dharma transmission from Zen Master Man'gong. In 1931 he became the head priest of Tongdo Temple; throughout his life he was given important posts in many Zen centers and temples of Korea. Revered to this day as being an example for all monks to follow and for his exceptional Buddhist wisdom, Zen Master Chŏn'gang died after completing a dharma lecture in January of 1975.

Zen Master Chinje

The head priest of Tonghwa Temple in Kyŏngbuk Province, Zen Master Chinje was born in 1931 in Namhae and was ordained in 1954. He founded Haeunjŏng Temple in 1971. In that year, he became head priest of Sŏnhagwŏn Zen Center.

Zen Master Hyeam

The 10th Supreme Patriarch of the Chogye Order, Zen Master Hyeam was born in Jangseong, Chŏnnam Province in 1920 and was ordained at Haein Temple in 1946. From then on, he ate only one meal a day. In 1993, he became head priest of Haein Temple after Zen Master Sŏngch'ŏl entered nirvana. A Zen Master in the Korean tradition of austere practice, Zen Master Hyeam died in Haein Temple December 31, 2001.

Zen Master Kobong

Zen Master Kobong was born in Taegu in 1890. After he attained enlightenment, he participated in the Korean independence movement against the Japanese colonial regime. He served as Abbot of Ŭnjŏk Hermitage within Magok Temple in Kongju, Ponggok Temple in Kongju, Pokchŏn Hermitage in Taejon, and Mit'a Temple in Seoul. Zen Master Kobong died in 1961.

Zen Master Kosong

Zen Master Kosong was born in 1906 in Yŏngch'ŏn, Kyŏngbuk Province and was ordained in 1920 at P'agye Temple of Mt. P'algong. He is remembered for practicing Zen more than eighty years but never accepting any position as a high official, and he was never involved in any strife. Master Kosong died September 22, 2003.

Zen Master Kyŏngbong

Ordained in 1907 at the age of fifteen, Master Kyŏngbong was born in Miryang, Kyŏngnam Province, in 1892. Master Kyŏngbong was Abbot of T'ongdo Temple in Yangsang, one of the most important temples of the Chogye Order in Korea. At T'ongdo Temple, Master Kyŏngbong became famous for the many monks he taught. After turning ninety, Master Kyŏngbong began to give dharma lectures, which more than one thousand people would regularly attend. In 1982, Master Kyŏngbong wrote his last lecture, "Touch the Crossbar at Midnight," and died.

Zen Master Man'gong

Zen Master Man'gong was born in Chŏngop, Chŏnbuk Province in 1871 and was ordained at the age of fourteen. Except for three years' Zen teaching in Mahayeon Temple in Kŭmgang Mountain and serving shortly as Abbot of Magok Temple, he spent most of his life teaching Zen at Dŏksung Mountain in Yesan, Ch'ungnam Province. He has been regarded as one of the greatest Zen Masters of Korea who revitalized the Zen tradition of Korean Buddhism along with his teacher, Zen Master Kyŏng-hŏ. Zen Master Man'gong died in 1946.

Zen Master Muksan

Master Muksan was born on Cheju Island in 1922. Beginning in 1959, he served as an assistant to Master In'gok, Abbot of Haein Temple. In 1975 he established Porim Zen Center in Seoul, where, on every Saturday since 1996, he has taught laypersons how to practice Zen through an entire night.

Zen Master Posŏng

Zen Master Posŏng was born in Sŏngju, Kyŏngbuk Province in 1928 and became the 5th Abbot of Song-gwang Temple in 1973. As a Master of the precepts, he has emphasized the importance of Buddhist tenets, and maintains that Buddhism is not learning or a discourse but a practice.

Zen Master Sŏam

Zen Master Sŏam was born in 1914 and was ordained at Soak Temple of Yech'on in 1935. He was Secretary General and Chairman of the Board of Elders of the Chogye Order. He was head priest of Pongam Temple and the 9th Supreme Patriarch of the Chogye Order. Master Sŏam died March 29, 2003.

Zen Master Sŏkchu

Zen Master Sŏkchu was born in 1923 in Andong, Kyŏngbuk Province and was ordained at Sŏnhagwŏn Zen Center. He served as Abbot of Pulguk Temple and Unhye Temple. Twice Secretary General of the Chogye Order, Master Sŏkchu died November 14, 2004.

Zen Master Sŏngsu

The head priest of Hwangdae Zen Center at Mt. Hwangseok in Kyŏngnam Province, Zen Master Sŏngsu was born in 1923 in Ulju, Kyŏngnam Province. He was ordained at Naewon Temple in Pusan in 1944. Once Secretary General of the Chogye Order, Master Sŏngsu now leads Hwangdae Zen Center in Hamyang, Kyŏngnam Province.

Zen Master Sŏong

The head priest of Paegyang Temple and the 5th Supreme Patriarch of the Chogye Order, Zen Master Sŏong was born in 1912 in Nonsan, Ch'ungnam Province and was ordained in 1932. He died in 2003 at the age of 92.

Zen Master Sungsan

Zen Master Sungsan was born in Sunch'ŏn, P'yŏngnam Province in 1927, and was ordained in Magok Temple. He received dharma transmission from Zen Master Kobong, was the head priest of Hwagye Temple, and he established international Zen centers in Hong Kong, the United States, Canada, Brazil, France, and Singapore. Master Sungsan died November 30, 2004.

Zen Master Taewŏn

Zen Master Taewŏn was born in 1936 and was ordained at Haein Temple in 1954 by Zen Master In'gok. In 1961 he received transmission from Zen Master Chŏn'gang and began teaching at Pohyŏn Temple, a meditation hall for laypeople. Currently, Master Taewŏn is devoted to teaching his disciples in Zen centers he has established in Seoul, Busan, and Kwangju, and the translation of Buddhist sutras and texts by patriarchs.

Zen Master Wŏndam

The head priest of Sudŏk Temple, Zen Master Wondam was born in 1926 in Okku, Chŏnnam Province, and was ordained in 1937. He succeeded Zen Master Mangong to become Abbot of Sudŏk Temple.

Dictionary of Terms

ANCIENT BUDDHA: Refers to the egoless original nature.

DHARMA: The underlying order in nature and human life; consequently, it is behavior considered to be in accord with that order. Ethically, it means "right way of living." With respect to spirituality, dharma might be considered a way for living higher truths.

A DROP OF THE CHOGYE STREAM: The temple the Sixth Patriarch of Chogye Buddhism lived in had a stream in front of it. To drink "a drop of the Chogye stream" means to understand the Sixth Patriarch's dharma.

EMPTY AND SERENE STATE: The realm of consciousness where there is not even the origin of causation.

"I DON'T KNOW" KOAN: Emperor Mu of the Yang Dynasty asked the Great Master Boddhidharma, "Who is facing me?" Boddhidharma said, "I don't know."

"JUST LIKE THIS": "As it is" life, where daily life is the embodiment of enlightenment.

KIMCH'I: A traditional Korean fermented dish made of select vegetables with varied seasonings, most commonly made of cabbage.

KOAN: A problem set by a Zen Master to help a practitioner gain wisdom.

MAITREYA: Maitreya is generally believed by Buddhists to be the one who will eventually appear on Earth, achieve complete enlightenment, and teach pure dharma. In Zen Buddhism, Maitreya can also refer to one who has enlightenment.

NAMJŎN KILLS A CAT: When Master Namjŏn was alive, monks of east and west factions fought over a cat. Namjŏn held the cat up in one hand and a knife in the other and shouted, "Answer me now. If you say the right answer, I'll set this cat free. But if you do not, I will cut it in half." The monks didn't say a word. Namjŏn cut the cat in half. The koan is, "What should they have done to set the cat free?"

MOKT'AG: A wooden block, usually hollow, struck while chanting.

OMI TEA: A cold tea in which all five flavors can be tasted: sweet, sour, salty, bitter, and pungent.

SAMSARA: The eternal cycle of reincarnation.

SWORD IN A DREAM: Wisdom which unenlightened people use.

TEN DIRECTIONS: North, south, east, west, the four directions in between, and up and down.

THE FOUR ELEMENTS: Earth, water, fire, air.

THREE PERIODS: Past, present, and future.

"THREE POUNDS OF HEMP" KOAN: A monk once visited Zen Master Tongsan and asked, "What is the Buddha?" Master Tongsan answered, "Three pounds of hemp."

The Editor and Translators

Ian Haight (editor): Ian Haight is an award winning poet and translator. For more information please visit ianhaight.com.

Park, Hongjin (translator) is a graduate of Seoul National University School of Law, and Deputy Director of the Korean Ministry of Strategy and Finance.

Eryn Michael Reager (translator) was ordained as a Zen monk in both Thailand and Korea (1994, 1995). Currently he is a nurse at Oregon University of Health Sciences.